THE Columbia;

Powerhouse of North America

by JEAN LEE LATHAM

Map by Fred Kliem

GARRARD PUBLISHING COMPANY
CHAMPAIGN, ILLINOIS

NANCY LARRICK, ED.D.,
IS THE EDUCATIONAL ADVISOR FOR THIS SERIES

For reading the manuscript of this book and checking the accuracy of its content, the author and the editor are grateful to Bruce Mitchell, Research Director of the Chelan County Industrial Development Council, Inc., Wenatchee, Washington, and to the Engineering staff of Bonneville Power Administration, United States Department of the Interior.

Manufactured in the U.S.A.
Library of Congress Catalog Card Number: 67-10022

Bureau of Reclamation

A homestead abandoned before Columbia water reached the dry land.

Contents

Oregon State Highway Department

The new highway bridge at Astoria, near the mouth of the Columbia.

1. The River That Lost Its Name

Before there was a United States, men in America had heard of a great River of the West. Indians said it rose in the Rocky Mountains and flowed to the Pacific Ocean. They called it the Oregon River.

Captain James Cook, the great British explorer, scoured the northwest coast in 1778, but he did not find the river. He died on that voyage. His men took the sad news back to England. They had other news, too: there was a fortune in furs on that coast.

Soon ships of three nations—Russia, Spain, and Great Britain—swarmed up and down the northwest coast. After the American Revolution, the new nation sent its ships out, too. Sea captains traded for the skins of sea otter—and explored. Those early sea captains always explored. Perhaps

Culver Pictures Inc.

This ship, the Columbia, gave its name to the river.

they would find a passage through America. If not that, they might at least find a river never before visited by any civilized nation. (To them the Indians did not count.) If a captain found such a river, he would claim the river and all the land it drained for his country.

Years passed. Then, in 1792, white men found the River of the West. In less than six months men of both Britain and America entered the river. That fact started an argument that lasted for over 50 years.

Early in 1792 Captain Robert Gray of Boston was on the northwest coast. His ship, the *Columbia,* was the pride of Boston, for she was the first American ship to sail around the world.

One morning Captain Gray studied the coastline through his spyglass. He saw signs of a river—a big river. Water of a different color was pouring into the sea from between a cape on the north and a long sandspit on the south.

The sea was too rough for him to venture near the shore. He waited . . . and waited . . . for nine days, but the sea was still too rough.

So he sailed north, where he met up with Captain George Vancouver and a squadron of three British ships. Captain Gray told Captain Vancouver about the river and where he was sure it was.

Later, Captain Gray sailed down the coast again. This time the sea was not so rough. He found the mouth of the river and sailed into it. He named it Columbia's River for his ship, but men soon called it just the Columbia River.

Captain Gray stayed in the mouth of the river for a few days, trading with the Indians for furs.

Then he sailed up the river a few miles, exploring. When he started downriver again to the sea, he went aground on a sandbar. It took him a week to find his way through sandbars and out to sea again.

Historians differ about the Gray-Vancouver meeting. Some say they met only before Gray entered the river. Some say they met afterward. At any rate, in October 1792, Captain Vancouver sent a ship under Lieutenant Broughton to hunt for the river. Broughton found it and explored it for over 100 miles in a boat.

When Captain Vancouver got home, he made a report on his voyage and told of the river. He said that since men of no civilized nation had been there before, he had taken possession in the name of the King of England.

Did Captain Vancouver believe his ship was the first in the river? History can't answer that question. But history can take note of a fact: Three years later, in 1795, a British map located the river—and called it the Columbia.

For the River of the West had lost its name.

Culver Pictures Inc.

Captain Robert Gray, discoverer of the Columbia.

Men called the country in the region of the river —including what is today British Columbia, Washington, Oregon, Idaho, and parts of Montana and Wyoming—"Oregon Country." But the river that the Indians called the Oregon had become the Columbia.

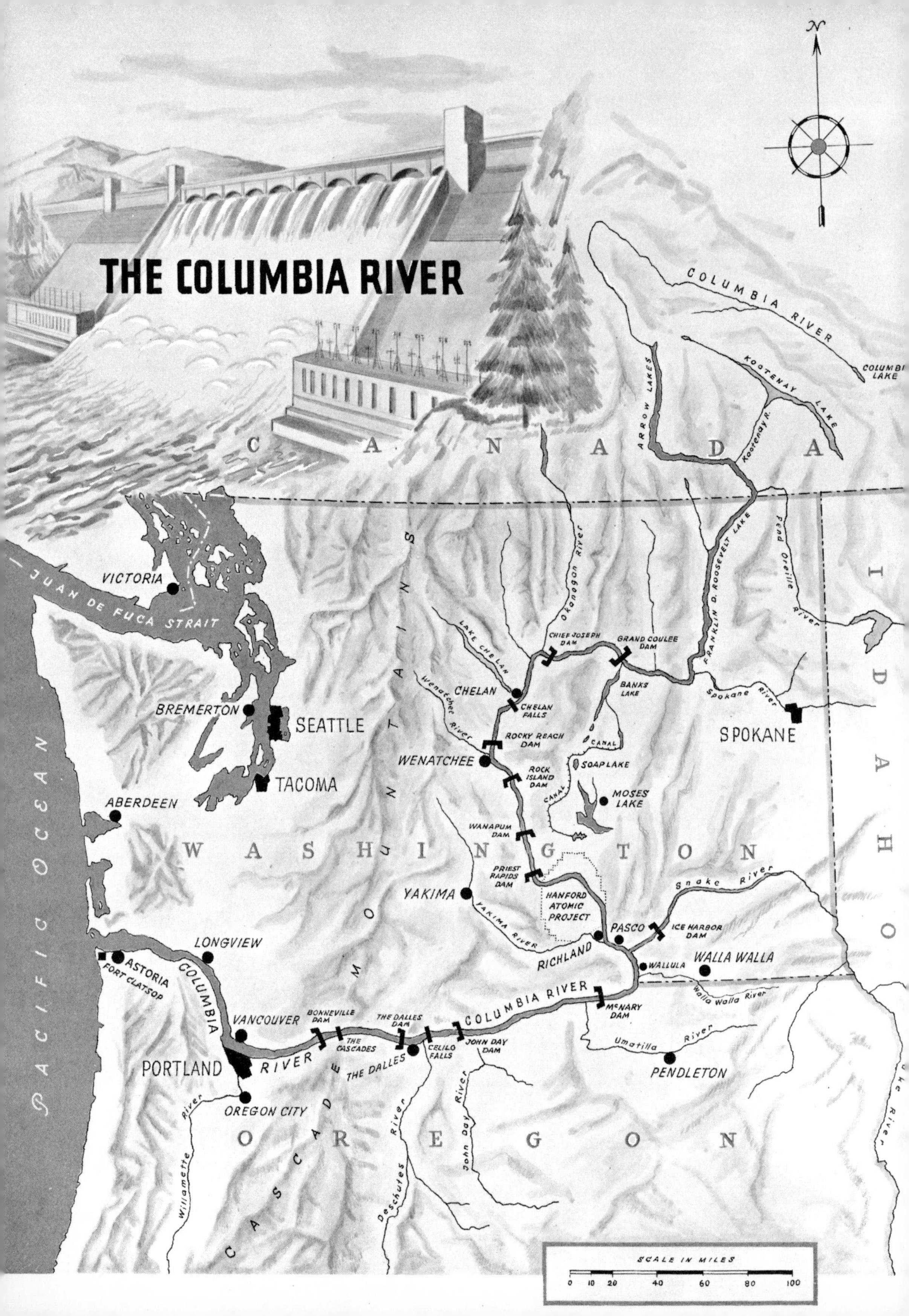
THE COLUMBIA RIVER
CANADA
COLUMBIA RIVER
COLUMBIA LAKE
KOOTENAY LAKE
Kootenay R.
ARROW LAKES
FRANKLIN D. ROOSEVELT LAKE
Pend Oreille River
JUAN DE FUCA STRAIT
VICTORIA
Okanogan River
CHIEF JOSEPH DAM
GRAND COULEE DAM
LAKE CHELAN
CHELAN
CHELAN FALLS
BANKS LAKE
Spokane River
SPOKANE
BREMERTON
SEATTLE
Wenatchee River
ROCKY REACH DAM
WENATCHEE
CANAL
SOAP LAKE
ROCK ISLAND DAM
TACOMA
MOSES LAKE
ABERDEEN
WANAPUM DAM
WASHINGTON
IDAHO
PRIEST RAPIDS DAM
HANFORD ATOMIC PROJECT
Snake River
YAKIMA
Yakima River
PASCO
ICE HARBOR DAM
RICHLAND
WALLULA
WALLA WALLA
PACIFIC OCEAN
LONGVIEW
ASTORIA
FORT CLATSOP
COLUMBIA
Walla Walla River
McNARY DAM
VANCOUVER
BONNEVILLE DAM
THE CASCADES
THE DALLES DAM
COLUMBIA RIVER
CELILO FALLS
JOHN DAY DAM
Umatilla River
PORTLAND
RIVER
THE DALLES
PENDLETON
OREGON CITY
CASCADE MOUNTAINS
Willamette River
Deschutes River
John Day River
OREGON
SCALE IN MILES
0 10 20 40 60 80 100

2. River of Two Nations

After 1792 both Britain and the United States claimed the Columbia River "and all the land it drained." Neither nation knew much about the river. Almost 20 years passed before a white man traced the course of the Columbia from its head-waters to its mouth.

In round numbers, the Columbia is 1,200 miles long: almost 500 miles are in the Canadian province of British Columbia where it rises; over 700 miles are in the United States. The part in British Columbia makes an upside-down U. At first the river flows north, hemmed in between the Rocky Mountains and the Selkirk Mountains. Then it makes the Big Bend around the northern end of the Selkirks and flows south. Finally, it enters the United States.

For about 100 miles it flows south and a bit west in the state of Washington. Then its course takes the shape of a top-heavy **S**, with a long tail. The loops of the top-heavy **S** are in Washington. The tail makes the boundary between Washington and Oregon.

The headwaters of the river are more than half a mile above sea level, so the Columbia plunges over cliffs, boils through rapids, roars through chasms hundreds of feet deep, and wears a channel through the Cascade Mountains on its thunderous course to the sea.

It cuts through beds of black lava from ancient volcanoes. It cuts away softer rock and swirls around huge boulders left in its path.

Those black rocks reminded early Frenchmen of paving stones back home, so they called them *dalles*, the French word for slabs or tiles. Any part of the Columbia named *The Dalles* was dangerous. One stretch in British Columbia is called *Dalles du Mort*—Dalles of Death, or Death Rapids.

That was the unknown river that men would explore, struggle with, die in, and finally try to tame. But as yet they knew little about it. They just claimed it.

British Columbia Government

The source of the Columbia, in the mountains of British Columbia.

Most Americans were not interested in the country of the Columbia, because it was too far away. At that time the United States owned no land west of the Mississippi River. Then, in 1803, President Jefferson bought the Louisiana Territory.

The territory began at the mouth of the Mississippi River and spread northwestward in a huge wedge. Nobody knew just how far west it spread or how far north it went. But at least it reached from the Mississippi to the Rocky Mountains. Now the Columbia River did not seem so far away.

That very year President Jefferson sent Lewis and Clark to explore the lands west of the Mississippi. They were to cross the Louisiana Territory, cross the Rocky Mountains, find the Columbia River and follow it to the sea.

They found the Columbia River, all right, and followed it to the sea. But they saw less than 350 miles of its course, because they entered it from the Snake River.

Soon they were fighting their way through rapids. They heard a thunderous roar as they neared the Celilo Falls.

Indians were standing on the banks of the river. These Indians of the Columbia looked nothing like the Indians of the plains. The Plains Indians practically lived on horseback, riding hard and long as they hunted for their food. They were generally tall, lean, and well built. The Indians of the Columbia did not have to ride long and hard hunting for food. The river gave them their chief food —salmon. They spent much of their lives in big dugout canoes made of cedar, or fishing from the banks of the river. They were generally short, with heavy ankles and flat feet.

Now the Indians above Celilo Falls were fishing with spears and nets, catching huge salmon.

The white men stared with their mouths open at the salmon in that torrent of water. For the salmon were leaping *upstream* against it.

Lewis and Clark were seeing one step in the amazing life history of the salmon. Baby salmon are hatched from eggs laid in fresh water, far from the sea. After a season or two they leave the place where they were born and swim down to the sea. After four or five years the adult salmon

Royal Ontario Museum, Toronto

Paul Kane's painting shows Indians fishing for salmon at Colville.

come back upstream to lay their eggs. They swim against the rapids, leap up the falls, and fight their way back to the very place where they were born, often hundreds of miles from the sea. There they lay their eggs, start a new generation, and die.

As the salmon came upstream, the Indians caught them, split them, dried them, pounded the flesh to powder, and packed it in big baskets.

Now the white men saw millions of salmon,

leaping the falls, struggling in nets, and drying on racks. At first, fresh-caught salmon tasted delicious. But before the white men reached the Pacific, they had eaten so much salmon that they never wanted to see another fish.

Lewis and Clark left the Indian fishermen, dragged their boats around stretches of the river that were too dangerous, and fought their way through other rapids and whirlpools. At the mouth of the Columbia, they built Fort Clatsop—named for an Indian tribe—and settled down for the winter.

This was strange country. East of Celilo Falls everything had been dry and barren. Here on the coast it rained and rained. In five months they had just ten days of sunshine. They spent the winter with soggy blankets—and fleas.

In 1806 Lewis and Clark got back home. The story of their travels was not going to encourage a great migration west, but America's claim to the Oregon Country had been strengthened.

It was time, President Jefferson thought, for Americans to do something about that vast region, or they might lose their claim on it. Great Britain was not sending settlements into the country, but her fur traders were moving farther and farther west. If Oregon Country were dotted with British fur trading posts, it might be hard for Americans to gain a toehold in the country.

There were two British fur companies in Canada —bitter rivals. The Hudson's Bay Company was controlled by men in London. The Northwest Company was owned by merchants of Canada. The Nor'westers were the fur traders who were moving into the West.

In 1810 a man of New York City decided to challenge the Nor'westers. He had the vision and the money to do it. This was John Jacob Astor, who had already founded the American Fur Company. Now he decided he would found the Pacific Fur Company and send men to build a fur trading post at the mouth of the Columbia River. From there, his ships could sail to China and make him a fortune selling furs. From there, too, his men could go inland, up the Columbia and its tributaries, and found other trading posts.

Amon Carter Museum, Fort Worth

Lewis and Clark on the Columbia, as painted by Charles M. Russell.

That was not all of his dream. He hoped to make a business arrangement with the Russians in Alaska. Soon he would be the power behind the greatest fur trading company in the world. And he would save the Oregon Country for the United States.

3. Mr. Astor vs. the British

In 1810 John Jacob Astor sent out two expeditions to the Far West. The first, under Wilson Price Hunt, was to go overland, through the Louisiana Territory, across the Rocky Mountains, and down the Columbia to the sea. On the way, Mr. Hunt was to search for possible places to locate inland trading posts. The second expedition, under Alexander McKay and Duncan McDougall, was to go by sea, from New York around Cape Horn on the southern tip of South America, then north to the mouth of the Columbia River, and set up the first trading post. Their ship was the *Tonquin*, commanded by Captain Thorn.

McKay and McDougall were Nor'westers whom Mr. Astor had lured away by making them partners in his company with a share in the profits.

He hired other Nor'westers, too—French voyageurs. The French were fur traders in Canada before the British came. The voyageurs were skilled boatmen and trappers. They could paddle a canoe all day and dance to a fiddle all night.

The *Tonquin* sailed with fair winds and high spirits, but soon trouble was brewing. Captain Thorn was a martinet. He ruled his crew with an iron hand and tried to rule the fur traders the same way.

Soon the fur traders found a way to bedevil the captain. The voyageurs spoke French and the partners spoke Gaelic, the old language of Scotland. When they held long conversations the captain could not understand, he fumed.

On the way the *Tonquin* stopped briefly in the Sandwich Islands—called Hawaii today. From there the captain sent a letter back to Mr. Astor, saying the fur traders were a scurvy lot! He hired a few Kanakas—Hawaiian workmen—and took them along. They were good sailors.

Late in March 1811, the *Tonquin* arrived off the mouth of the Columbia River. The sea was as rough as it had been when Captain Gray had first been there in 1792. Captain Gray had waited nine days for calmer seas and then had sailed away.

But Captain Thorn was not a patient man. He ordered his chief mate, Mr. Fox, to take one sailor and three voyageurs in a boat to hunt for a channel. Mr. Fox pleaded for more able seamen. The voyageurs were used to rivers, but they were not used to handling a boat through raging seas. Captain Thorn would not listen.

The partners, McKay and McDougall, tried to reason with him, but the fur traders had bedeviled him too long. Captain Thorn stared at them coldly, then turned on his heel and barked the order, "Lower away the boat!"

The boat pitched and tossed, then disappeared in the mist. The day passed and night fell. No word from the boat. Morning dawned, gray and stormy. Another day passed. Another night. Another day dawned. Still no word from the boat.

The third morning the sea was not quite so rough. Twice another boat tried to reach the shore, but had to turn back. In the afternoon the

Historical Pictures Service, Chicago

An oldtime trapper and his skins, portrayed by Frederic Remington.

captain sent out a boat once more, manned by three of his crew and two Kanakas.

This time the boatmen found the channel. They signaled the good news, then started back to the ship. But a sudden squall struck their boat, driving it toward the shore. It disappeared.

The next day brought sunshine and a calmer sea. The *Tonquin* found her way through the channel and anchored. Men landed and scoured the coast in both directions. They finally found two men who had been in the second boat that was lost. They found no sign of either of the lost boats, or any other survivors. Eight men had paid with their lives for one man's impatience.

After that, McKay and McDougall must have hoped that Captain Thorn had learned his lesson and would be more reasonable. He was not. He fumed over the delay while the partners hunted for a place to build their trading post. Not until April 12 did they find the spot. They named it Astoria. Then they set to work to put up houses for shelter and a storehouse for their supplies.

It was June 1 before the *Tonquin* could leave the Columbia and sail up the coast to trade for furs. Then a storm delayed the start till June 5. By the time the *Tonquin* got under way, Thorn's mood was blacker than the skies had been.

At his first stop, Captain Thorn picked up an Indian named Lamazee who knew a little English and could act as interpreter. Then the captain ordered the *Tonquin* to make for a port on Vancouver Island. Lamazee warned him. It was not safe! The Indians there were fierce and treacherous.

Captain Thorn said "Humph!" He put in at the port. The Indians came to trade, and Captain Thorn spread his wares. He told them how many otter skins they must give for a blanket.

But the Indian chief laughed at Captain Thorn.

"Softly!" Lamazee whispered. "Bargain with him!"

But Thorn was in no mood to bargain with a savage. He snatched a skin from the chief's hand, rubbed it on his face, kicked the furs about, and ordered the Indians off the ship. They went—but the chief's eyes were blazing.

Lamazee groaned. The *Tonquin* must not stay here! She must sail immediately!

The captain snorted. Tomorrow the Indians would be back. They would be ready to trade.

Early next morning the watchman on the *Tonquin* smiled. There came Indian canoes by the dozens, loaded with furs! The Indians were even wearing short fur capes. Perhaps they would trade them, too.

By the time the captain was stirring, the deck was jammed with Indians. Lamazee pleaded with the captain. It was not safe! Did he see those capes? The Indians could be hiding knives under them.

The captain turned his back on Lamazee.

Just then the Indian chief yelled. At the signal, all the Indians whipped out knives and war clubs hidden under their capes. The white men did not have a chance.

Five men escaped below deck. One, a Mr. Lewis, was mortally wounded. The other four managed to break open a chest and get guns. They fired up through the hatch, and the yelling Indians left the ship. The four men crept on deck. Not another man of the *Tonquin*'s crew was alive. Lamazee had disappeared. Was he dead, a prisoner, or had he deserted?

The four men could not handle the ship. They waited until dark, then launched a boat to try to escape.

Lewis refused to go with them. "It's no use," he said. "I'm going to die, but I'll take a lot of those devils with me when I go!"

The next morning canoes surrounded the ship. Warily, then more sure of themselves, the Indians swarmed on board. They began to toss trading goods down to other Indians waiting in the canoes.

Suddenly there was a *boom.* The powder room of

the *Tonquin* had exploded. The blast killed every Indian on board, and killed or wounded many in the nearby canoes. Mr. Lewis had kept his vow.

The men at Astoria knew nothing of the fate of the *Tonquin* until Lamazee came to the post with

Plowing and fence-building in Oregon, as drawn by W. A. Rogers.
Historical Pictures Service, Chicago

the news. He had been captured by the Indians and had finally escaped. No white man on the *Tonquin* had lived. The four who tried to escape in the boat had been caught and put to death by slow torture.

Gloom hung over the Astorians. The *Tonquin* had been lost with all hands, and they had heard nothing of Mr. Hunt and the overland party.

One day a glad shout went up. A boat was coming down the Columbia. Mr. Hunt's party at last!

But instead of the overland party, it was David Thompson, the great geographer and astronomer of the Nor'westers. This was the man who had explored and mapped over a million square miles of the Northwest. McKay and McDougall pumped his hand and slapped him on the back. They were with different companies now, but Thompson was a prince of a fellow. Everybody liked him. Did he have any news?

Soon every Astorian sat motionless, listening. Pipes went out and were forgotten. Nobody moved. David Thompson had done what no white man had done before. He had traveled the Columbia from its headwaters to Astoria. He told of the headwaters—of a quiet lake between towering cliffs, and then of its headlong rush to the sea—wild torrents plunging over falls and through rapids.

He had other news, too. Soon the Astorians were shooting sidelong glances at each other. The Nor'westers were setting up trading posts west of the Rockies.

So . . . the struggle between the Americans and the British was about to begin!

McKay and McDougall sent men to set up other fur trading posts inland. That left them very short-handed at Astoria. One day a friendly Indian brought a warning: Indians from the north were planning to attack Astoria.

The Indians came. They prowled about the place, evidently sizing up the situation. Mr. McDougall had an inspiration. He showed the Indians a corked bottle. That, he said, was full of smallpox spirits. If the Indians made trouble, he would open the bottle and let loose the spirits of smallpox upon them. The Indians fled. Mr. McDougall smiled and dusted his hands. That had settled that!

At last the overlanders reached Astoria, and in the spring of 1812, another supply ship came. It brought 30 more men—Americans this time. The Astorians went around with smiles; everything was fine now.

It was the fall of 1812 before the Astorians learned that the United States and Great Britain were at war, and had been since June. Mr. McDougall paced the floor, worrying about it. What would happen to Astoria? He knew the British could blockade the whole east coast. Mr. Astor would not be able to send any more supply ships to his fur trading posts. What should he do? Finally he planned to buy horses from the Indians east of the Cascade Mountains and to escape overland with all the furs the horses could carry. But the other partners would not go along with his plan.

In the fall of 1813, ten canoes filled with Nor'-westers came down the Columbia. Their leader, John G. McTavish, gave the Astorians grim news. British warships were in the Pacific. One might reach the Columbia River any day. He let that fact sink in, then made his offer. He would buy out the

Oregon State Highway Department

A net used in salmon fishing is dried at a wharf in Astoria.

trading post at Astoria and hire all the men who wanted work. Wouldn't it be better to sell out to him than to lose everything to a British warship?

McDougall agreed. He sold out.

The War of 1812 ended in a stalemate, with nothing settled. Astoria was finally returned to Mr. Astor, but the United States could not promise protection to such a far-off place, so Mr. Astor let the Nor'westers run it.

4. The White-Headed Eagle

The War of 1812 left many questions unsettled. For instance, who owned the Oregon Country? Britain had no use for it, except for the fur trade. There was a fortune in furs—sea otter on the coast and beaver and other furs inland. Americans, as a whole, were not interested in the region. Eastern statesmen said it was too far away to settle. Why not give up the Oregon Country? It would be better to bargain with the British for something worth having.

Finally, in 1818, Great Britain and the United States agreed on joint occupancy of the Oregon Country. Men of both nations could trade and trap there. They could even settle there—if anybody wanted to.

Not long after this agreement, the Nor'westers

Oregon Historical Society
Mrs. John McLoughlin

Historical Pictures Service, Chicago
Dr. John McLoughlin

combined with their ancient rivals, the Hudson's Bay Company. That meant that the London owners of the Hudson's Bay Company controlled Oregon Country. It was a vast territory, from south of Alaska to north of California, and from the Rocky Mountains to the Pacific Ocean. The company needed a strong man to be chief factor and rule over all their trading posts.

They chose Dr. John McLoughlin, a Canadian. For 21 years, from 1824 to 1845, McLoughlin was king of Oregon Country. He was a 6-foot 4-inch giant of a man. Although he was not quite 40 when he took charge, he had a mane of white hair. Indians called him the White-Headed Eagle. Indians and white men—Scotsmen, English, and

French voyageurs—all came under his rule. They might or might not like him, but they all respected him.

McLoughlin had two orders from the company: Make a profit in the fur trade. Keep out American fur traders. (Do that politely, of course! After all, there *was* the matter of joint occupancy!)

McLoughlin soon revolutionized the trading post. He left the run-down quarters that had been Astoria, built a new post 114 miles upriver, and named it Fort Vancouver.

The new post was no rough shelter for half-savage, roistering men. A palisade enclosed a rectangle 500 by 750 feet. Inside were more than 40 sturdy buildings—bachelors' quarters, a stone powder house, storehouses, a hospital and a school. The factor's house was a great mansion of logs, two stories high, with quarters for the factor and his family, a visitors' hall, and a great hall where more than 50 men often sat down to dine.

Word of Fort Vancouver spread far and wide. Here was civilization in the wilderness. Dr. McLoughlin had a good library and even had the

London *Times* sent to him by every company ship that sailed.

But he did not depend on company ships for supplies and food. He had gardens planted and brought cattle from California. Before long, nine square miles of farmland surrounded the fort. Outside the palisade there were a dairy and a forge to make knives and hatchets for the Indian trade. There were cottages for the married workmen and voyageurs.

McLoughlin allowed no rum in the Indian trade. Once he bought the whole cargo of rum from a ship and stowed it, unopened, in his cellar.

He insisted on the same justice for Indian and white man. Many of the fur traders had Indian wives. McLoughlin understood that because he had married the handsome widow of Alexander McKay of the Astorians. She was half Indian. He was true to his wife, and he insisted that his men be true to their Indian wives. If a man deserted his Indian wife, McLoughlin dismissed him in disgrace, and a man dismissed by McLoughlin found no place in Oregon Country. There was more than one

New York Public Library

Fort Vancouver, where the White-Headed Eagle ruled a vast domain.

reason why the Indians respected the White-Headed Eagle.

Presently the ten-year term of the joint occupancy agreement ran out. Americans still had no foothold in the country, but the British were satisfied with the way things were going. The agreement was renewed to run indefinitely. Either country could end it by giving a year's notice.

The White-Headed Eagle continued to rule. From time to time American fur traders came, and McLoughlin always welcomed them when they arrived. If they had had a hard trip, he took care of them. He often gave them supplies on credit. But their American trading posts failed. The Indians ignored the Americans and traded with the White-Headed Eagle.

Eight years passed under his rule. Then, in 1832, another type of American came to Oregon Country. The newcomers were missionaries who had been invited by the Indians. Often the Indians had seen white men with Bibles. David Thompson, the great geographer of the Nor'westers, always carried his Bible and talked with the Indians about his God. The White-Headed Eagle held services every Sunday at Fort Vancouver for all men—white and Indian.

Maybe, the Indians decided, there was Great Medicine in the white man's Bible. Two old chiefs remembered Lewis and Clark. They made a long journey to St. Louis to see William Clark and asked him to send them men with the Bible. Clark could not help them, but the story of their plea spread across America.

American missionaries began to come to Oregon Country. In 1836 the first white women crossed the United States to the Columbia River. One was Narcissa Whitman, wife of Dr. Marcus Whitman. The other was Mrs. Spalding, wife of another missionary. The White-Headed Eagle welcomed them and sheltered the women at Fort Vancouver while their husbands built their homes.

More Americans came and settled in Oregon Country. Dr. McLoughlin went to London to talk with the British. If they did not settle the country, he said, they would lose it to the Americans. The British laughed off his warning.

In 1843 the "great migration" of Americans began. The Oregon Trail was rutted deep with the wheels of covered wagons. As always, McLoughlin welcomed the newcomers, but he encouraged them to settle *south* of the Columbia River, in the Willamette Valley. True, it was the best farming land in the region. But McLoughlin had another reason. He believed that joint occupancy would end soon, and he hoped the Columbia would be the dividing line—that the United States would get the country south of the river, and Great Britain all the land north of the river.

By 1845 trouble was brewing. The British backers of the Hudson's Bay Company were angry with McLoughlin. They saw huge sums on his account books for goods charged to American settlers.

"They will pay it back," McLoughlin said. "And I cannot let people starve. If I turned my back on them, the Indians would rise against them. *That must not happen!*"

But the backers in London fumed.

The American settlers were getting restless, too. They were tired of living under one man's rule. A fine thing for men who had won their independence from the British!

Moreover—and this worried McLoughlin—the Indians were growing sullen. Fur traders were all right. They used the land as the Indians did, hunting and trapping. They did not destroy it. But these settlers were overrunning the country like a blight, cutting down trees and planting fields.

There was another reason for the Indians' resentment. White men brought diseases that were new to the Indians. A sickness that might be a minor thing for a white person could wipe out a whole Indian village. The Indians had long memories. They had never forgotten McDougall and his smallpox bottle.

In 1846 joint occupancy ended. The boundary was settled where it is now. The United States got all the land south of the 49th parallel except Vancouver Island which went to the British. The Hudson's Bay Company moved its post to the island. The United States Army took over Fort Vancouver.

Things had come to a head between McLoughlin and the company. He had resigned and moved to Oregon City on the Willamette River. There were 500 people in Oregon City. It was the biggest city in the Oregon Country.

Now McLoughlin's firm control of the Indians was gone. He worried about their growing resentment. He sent word to the Whitmans at their far-off mission east of the Cascade Mountains. He begged them to give up the mission and come to Oregon City where they would be safer. The Whitmans thanked their old friend for his concern, but refused to leave the mission.

Historical Pictures Service, Chicago

A measles epidemic caused the assassination of Dr. Marcus Whitman.

In 1847 an epidemic of measles broke out around the Whitman mission. Dr. Whitman worked night and day to save Indians and whites, but more Indians died than white people. Then a rumor spread—Dr. Whitman had a measles bottle. He was killing off Indians with it. The long resentment of the Indians flared. They attacked the Whitman mission and killed both the Whitmans and twelve other people. That was the beginning of long and bitter wars between white men and Indians in the Northwest.

5. The Army vs. the Columbia

The Indian Wars of the Northwest began in 1847. They flared up time and again for 30 years. In 1877 the last Indian leader surrendered. He was Chief Joseph of the Nez Percé Indians, a great and tragic figure whom men could not forget. Chief Joseph Dam on the Columbia is named for him.

In those 30 years many changes had come to the United States. The Mexican War had added more land. Now America spread from ocean to ocean, and from the Rio Grande to Canada.

Oregon Territory was changing, too. In 1860 the Pony Express began. Men no longer had to wait two or three months for letters from the East. They could get them in days—if they could pay the rate. At first it cost five dollars for half an ounce; later, only a dollar. But the Pony Express drew East and West closer together.

In 1861 the telegraph reached from coast to coast and carried news even faster. The telegraph ruined the Pony Express. But it, too, drew East and West together.

In 1869 the Union Pacific Railroad spanned the country. Men going to the Far West no longer had to travel by covered wagon. They no longer had to make the long and dangerous route around Cape Horn at the tip of South America, or the shorter but equally dangerous voyage across Panama. They could cross the United States by train in about two weeks.

All these changes brought new settlers to the Northwest. By 1850 Portland had 800 people. It had passed Oregon City in population and was the largest city of the Northwest.

After 1850 population boomed in the Northwest: 13,000 in 1850; 63,000 in 1860; 115,000 in 1870 and double that number before 1880.

The fur trade was not the only business. White men were fishing for salmon on the Columbia; they had built a commercial cannery at Astoria. Lumbermen cut trees and floated them down the

Culver Pictures Inc.

Celilo Falls stopped steamboats, but not the Columbia's salmon.

Columbia. Farmers were raising cattle and wheat in the high country east of the Cascade Mountains.

Everything was changing but the river. It still foamed through rapids, roared over falls, dashed through canyons, and poured into the ocean.

By the 1850's there were steamboats on the Columbia. They could travel upriver as far as the Cascades. That was the end of the line for a steamboat. Above there, at Celilo Falls, the Columbia plunges down more than 80 feet. The early explorers had portaged, or carried, their canoes and supplies around these stretches of the river they could not navigate. In the 1860's men built portage railroads to carry passengers and supplies around such stretches of river above the Cascades. Then passengers could travel from Portland on the Willamette River to Wallula, on the Columbia. It was a distance of a little over 200 miles. A passenger could make the journey in two days and a night, by taking three different boats and two portage railroads.

He boarded the first boat at Portland before 5 A.M. and went as far as the Cascades. There he left the boat and boarded a portage railroad that took him around the rapids. Above the Cascades he left the railroad and boarded a second boat. By suppertime he reached The Dalles where he spent the night. At dawn the next morning he boarded a second railroad to get around Celilo Falls. Then he left that railroad and boarded the third boat, which reached Wallula by suppertime, with luck—good luck.

By 1877 the United States Army had tamed the warring Indians of the Northwest. Then the Army

Engineers began to tame the Columbia River to make navigation safer.

Seagoing ships could enter the Columbia and sail upriver to the Willamette River. They could enter the Willamette and sail on to the city of Portland. So that city, two rivers removed from the ocean, became a great port.

But the lower Columbia was a graveyard of ships. Many a ship missed the channel and went aground on treacherous sandbars. The Army Engineers began their work by dredging the mouth of the river to make a safer channel.

In 1881 Lieutenant Thomas W. Symons of the Army Engineers explored the Columbia from the Canadian border to the Cascades, to decide where navigation could be improved. He studied Kettle Falls, 41 miles below the Canadian border, and knew that it was no place for a boat. Below there, he hired a bateau and Pierre Agare, an old voyageur who knew the river. After much talking, Pierre managed to get four young Indians for oarsmen. A Mr. Downing went along to help Lieutenant Symons map the river.

Oregon Historical Society

An 1867 train photographed on the portage railroad above The Dalles.

The white men probably did not know how they held their breath as they entered the first rapids—a mile of crosscurrents and eddies that threatened to crash the boat against huge boulders. When they were safely through, Symons let out a gasp of relief.

Old Pierre smiled. "That's not bad. Kalichen Falls worse." They were about 180 miles downriver from the border when they heard a low rumble. Pierre nodded. "Kalichen Falls. Coming."

The Indians stopped the boat and listened to Pierre's words. Symons studied the men. Were they a little pale under the coppery cast of their skin? The young Indians nodded to Pierre. They stripped off most of their clothes and pulled off their gloves. Then each tied a bright handkerchief tightly around his head.

Old Pierre smiled at the white men. "Upset here once," he said. "Sixteen men. Lost eight." Then he nodded to the oarsmen.

With a shout at every stroke, the Indians began the battle. They had to go fast to overcome the currents and eddies.

A huge rock loomed ahead. *They're going to hit it!* Symons thought. But Pierre shouted an order. Two oarsmen backed water; the other two pulled until it looked as though their oars would snap. Symons flinched as they passed the boulder, but they did pass it.

They passed the mouth of Chelan Creek, boiling into the river. (Chelan Creek dropped 400 feet in 2½ miles, so it is small wonder it surged into the Columbia.) The men were over 280 miles from the border when again they heard a deep rumble ahead.

"Rock Island Rapids," Pierre said.

This, Symons decided, was evidently going to be worse than Kalichen Falls. For the Indians pulled for the shore and dragged the boat up on the riverbank. Then they got out and went ahead on foot to study the rapids. At last they came back to the boat.

Once more the Indians stripped down and tied the bright kerchiefs around their heads. Suddenly it dawned on Symons what the kerchiefs were for. If the boat capsized, it would be easier to see a bright kerchief than a dark head.

Again the Indians yelled with every stroke in their breakneck speed through the Rock Island Rapids. At last they were safely past them.

"Stop now?" Pierre asked. "Make camp?"

"Yes!" Symons had not meant to sound so violent about it.

Old Pierre smiled.

U. S. Army Engineers

Three barges are pushed by a tug through the lock at McNary Dam.

When Symons had finished his survey, he made his report on navigation of the upper Columbia. In 552 miles a crew would have to make 80 miles of portages. The rest of the way, when the water was just right—not too high or too low—a boat could follow the river. It would take skill, a good eye, keen judgment . . . and luck.

The Army Engineers were studying the Cascades

now, to make an all-water route past them. They knew they could do it with canals and locks.

"But it's going to be a long job," one engineer said.

It was a long job. They had to build a stairway of locks—watertight boxes with gates in their ends. Then they had to dig two canals to lead to the locks, above and below the Cascades.

It was 1896 when the first steamboat went upstairs past the Cascades. It left the river and entered the lower canal. With water filling the first lock to the depth of water in the canal, the lower gate opened and the boat entered. The lower gate closed and water flowed in, filling the lock and raising the boat until it was high enough to enter the next lock. And so it climbed until it reached the level of the upper canal and steamed back into the Columbia River above the Cascades.

The Army Engineers had taken one step in taming the Columbia. There was a long road ahead of them before the Columbia became the Powerhouse of North America.

6. Power from Water

Somebody once said, "Science is the truths of God that man has found out." Step by step, man has found out about magnets and electricity. Very early, men discovered that a magnet would pick up iron. Today they call that invisible pulling force around a magnet the "magnetic field."

Later, men learned they could make a magnet out of a bar of ordinary iron. They wrapped an insulated wire around the bar and sent an electric current through the wire. As long as current flowed in the wire, the iron bar was a magnet, so they called it an electromagnet.

Next, scientists found they could make electricity with a magnet. If they turned a loop of copper wire between the ends of a horseshoe magnet, an electric charge built up in the wire. If they connected the two ends of the wire to a continuous circuit, electric current would flow. The more loops of wire they used, the stronger the current; the bigger the magnet, the stronger the current, too.

Those facts were the beginning of the development of the generator—the huge machine that makes electricity to light our homes, run machines, and do a thousand and one things we could not do at all without electricity.

The more wires, the stronger the current. Modern generators may weigh tons and have miles of fine wires. *The stronger the magnetic field, the stronger the current.* The magnet in a modern generator is often a monster doughnut of iron with heavy copper wire around it. When current flows through that heavy wire, a terrific magnetic field builds up. Men can turn either the miles of fine wire, the armature of a generator, or they can turn the magnetic field. Either way, they can make an electric charge build up.

But it takes a powerful machine to turn either part of a huge generator. In the 1880's Thomas Edison ran a small generator with a steam engine to furnish current for some of his new electric lights. Not long afterward, a man ran a small generator with a waterwheel. This was an early edition of a hydroelectric plant—one that makes electricity with the power of falling water. Our huge modern turbines are a great improvement on yesterday's waterwheel.

Waterpower is the cheapest way to make electricity. A steam engine must use up coal, oil, or gas to make steam. A hydroelectric plant does not use up the water. Instead, the water flows through the turbine, back to the river, and down to the ocean. There it evaporates in the heat of the sun, rises, forms clouds, and falls to the earth again as rain or snow.

Engineers tell us that the Columbia River has more waterpower than any river in North America. How do they measure the power of a river?

Scientists have found that 1 cubic foot of water, falling 14 feet in 1 second into the blades of a turbine, will make 1,000 watts of electricity—enough electricity to light ten 100-watt light bulbs. The amount of electricity a river can generate depends on two things: the volume of

British Columbia Government

The Columbia at Bull Mountain, near Wardner, British Columbia.

water and the "head," or height from which the water is falling. A dam across a river backs up the water to get those two things—volume and head.

Engineers often measure water in cubic feet. They measure the water flowing past a given place in cubic feet per second. They call it second-feet or write c.f.s. They generally measure large amounts of standing water in acre-feet. An acre-foot of water is 43,560 cubic feet—enough to

Chelan County Public Utility District

Rocky Reach Dam. White arrow (left) points to top of fish ladder.

cover an acre of land to a depth of one foot. The lake behind Grand Coulee Dam has over 9 million acre-feet of water.

Engineers measure electricity in kilowatts (each kilowatt is 1,000 watts) and in kilowatt hours (1,000 watts used for one hour). Recently they have invented a new term for vast amounts of

Harold Lanay

The fish ladder that salmon climb to get past the Columbia dams.

electricity—a gigawatt. A gigawatt is a million kilowatts. Gigawatt is an odd-sounding word, but it will save writing a lot of zeros.

Only three rivers in North America have a greater volume of water than the Columbia—the Mackenzie in Canada, the St. Lawrence which drains the Great Lakes between the United States and Canada, and the Mississippi in the United States. Each of them pours more water into the ocean, but none has such a head as the Columbia.

The headwaters of the Columbia River are over half a mile above sea level. As the river rushes down to the sea, it must descend 2,650 feet.

The falls and rapids in which Lieutenant Symons risked his neck were places where dams could be built someday. The falls and rapids he had to portage around were even better places for dams.

The first dam on the Columbia was not built until 1931, and the Army Engineers did not build it. It was built by the Puget Sound Light and Power Company, at the dread Rock Island Rapids, just south of Wenatchee, Washington.

In 1933 the Army Engineers began to build a dam below the thundering Cascades, about 160 miles above the mouth of the Columbia River. They named the dam Bonneville, after the army officer who had been an explorer and fur trader in the West.

Bradford Island stood in the river below the

Cascades. The engineers planned to build the dam on the two sides of the island. North, in the wider channel between the island and Washington, they would build a spillway to let water through when spring floods came. South, in the narrower part of the channel between the island and Oregon, they would build the powerhouse with generators and turbines to run them. They would also build a lock for ships to go through. For Bonneville was to be a multipurpose dam—one that would do several things.

The first step in building a dam on a river is to get rid of the river so men can have a dry place to work. If a river is not too big, men can dig a tunnel or canal and detour the river around the place where they are going to work. But there was no hope of detouring the Columbia. It poured 200,000 second-feet of water over the Cascades. In floods, more than one million second-feet of water roared down.

The engineers used what they call cofferdams to shut out the water as they worked in the north channel. The cofferdams were made of cribs, or boxes of heavy timber, 60 feet square and 70 feet high. Each crib had to be shaped on the bottom to fit exactly on the bed of the river where it would stand. When a crib was done, the engineers towed it to its place and filled it with rocks to sink it. They fastened all the cribs together with watertight joints, in the shape of a horseshoe along the north bank of the river. Then they pumped out the water in the area the cofferdam enclosed and began to dig down to bedrock. They had to excavate to 93 feet below sea level. When the spillway was done, it was 197 feet high, with gates big enough to let any flood through—18 gates, each 50 feet wide.

The engineers knew they could not detour all the volume of water in the north channel at one time into the narrower south channel. If they had tried to do that, the tremendous force of the river would have swept out the cofferdam. So they built the spillway in three steps. They shut out water from the first section, along the Washington shore, and built up part of that section. Then they removed the cofferdam and let the water flow

Chelan County Public Utility District

At Rocky Reach Dam, fish get an opportunity to study human beings.

through that section of the spillway. They built a second cofferdam to shut out water from the other half of the channel. When they had completed that half, they removed the cofferdam and let the water flow through that part of the channel. Again they shut out water from the first section and completed it. Now they could let the water

Chelan County Public Utility District

A helicopter helps build a transmission tower for Columbia power.

flow through the whole spillway while they worked on the narrower south channel.

Bonneville Dam had two special features that had not been used before: The navigation lock could lift ships higher than any lock at that time—from 30 to 70 feet. Only a few years before, engineers had used two locks to lift a ship 25 feet. The dam also provided for the migration of salmon.

There were passageways for the young salmon, the fingerlings, to swim down to the sea. There were fish ladders for the adult salmon to swim back upstream. The fish ladders were ramps, over 1,000 feet long and 40 feet wide, curving down from above the dam to the river below. Each step on the ramp is a tank six feet deep, and each step is one foot higher than the one below it. The water pouring over the fish ladders is deep enough for the fish to swim upstream.

The ten generators at Bonneville are guaranteed to furnish 518,000 kilowatts of electricity. But during World War II they sometimes furnished 565,000 kilowatts.

7. White Elephant

A newspaper article in 1918 started the talk about Grand Coulee Dam. But nature had prepared the way for the dam long ages before.

First, there was the age of volcanoes. Layer after layer of lava spread over the earth and cooled. Then came glaciers—rivers of ice, moving slowly down a slope. One glacier moved into the canyon where the Columbia flowed and dammed the river.

The Columbia had to change its course and cut a new channel. For long ages it wore the new channel down through layers of lava. Finally, the glacier began to melt, pouring more and more water into the river. The mighty river roared through its new channel, cutting it deeper and deeper.

At last the glacier that had dammed the channel melted, and the Columbia returned to its old riverbed. It left a great chasm, or coulee, from 1 to 4 miles wide, over 50 miles long, cut down through layers of black lava. Early explorers stood in the coulee, stared up at the towering black cliffs and shivered in spite of the heat. The one-time riverbed was a place of utter loneliness and desolation. It was the Grand Coulee.

The country south of Grand Coulee, in the upper bend of the top-heavy **S**, was desolate, too. The Columbia Basin was a world of sagebrush and sand where "even a jack rabbit had to carry a canteen to cross it." Some explorers noticed one thing though: The sagebrush was unusually sturdy. That suggested the soil was rich; all it needed was water.

A desert jack rabbit, caught without his canteen.

W. P. Taylor, U. S. Fish and Wildlife Service

In the early 1900's homesteaders came to the Columbia Basin. Some happened to come at a time of more than usual rainfall. Their crops flourished. This, they said, was the promised land. But soon the time of rain-enough ended. The homesteaders watched, heartsick, as their crops died. They tried anything and everything to bring water to their thirsty land. Men organized one company after another to pump water from deep wells or from some lake or river. But all the processes were too expensive. The companies failed and many farmers gave up and moved away.

The Columbia Basin was not the only thirsty land in the United States. The 100th meridian cuts through the Dakotas, Nebraska, Kansas, Oklahoma, and Texas. Much of the land west of the 100th meridian gets less than 10 inches of rain a year. It takes an average rainfall of 30 inches a year for most crops to flourish.

President Theodore Roosevelt was an Easterner, but he knew and cared about the West. In 1901 he said, "The western half of the United States would sustain a population greater than that of our whole country today if the waters that now run to waste were saved and used for irrigation."

In 1902 he signed the bill that created the Bureau of Reclamation. Its purpose was to save the water that went to waste and make it usable for irrigation.

Therefore, after 1902, both the Army Engineers and the Bureau of Reclamation built dams. The Army Engineers built dams intended especially for flood control and navigation. The Bureau of Reclamation built dams meant especially for irrigation.

In 1903 the Bureau's engineers studied the Columbia Basin. They found a million acres of rich land, needing only water for crops to flourish. There was the Columbia River with abundant water, but the water was out of reach, deep in a canyon. Was there any way to get the water to the land? The engineers surveyed and finally reported: Not practical. More farmers gave up and moved away.

Years passed. Then came the idea of Grand

Bureau of Reclamation

This house in the Columbia basin was abandoned when crops withered.

Coulee Dam. Hundreds of men helped in the fight for the dam. Three men will always be remembered for their special part in the fight: Billy Clapp, lawyer, who first outlined the idea; Rufus Woods, editor of the *Wenatchee World*, who kept the idea alive in print; Jim O'Sullivan, ex-college teacher, who organized the fight for the dam and gave years of his life to it.

Rufus Woods was not one to sit in his newspaper office in Wenatchee. He probably covered more territory and knew more people than any

Bureau of Reclamation

The same farm (as shown left) after Columbia water nourished it.

man in the region. One day in 1918 he stopped in the dusty little town of Ephrata, set down in the sagebrush and sand. He listened to Billy Clapp's idea, and wrote a story about it for his newspaper.

Books that mention Grand Coulee often state Rufus Woods' story appeared on page 1 with a banner headline:

TWO MILLION WILD HORSES!

But that famous headline appeared years later, in a picture of Woods holding a copy of the *Wenatchee*

World. The original story in July of 1918 appeared on page 7, with a factual headline:

FORMULATE BRAND NEW IDEA FOR IRRIGATION
GRANT, ADAMS, FRANKLIN COUNTIES
COVERING MILLION ACRES OR MORE

Rufus Woods knew his readers; that was the headline that would make them stop to read.

TWO MILLION WILD HORSES! is a magnificent headline, though. And it is the inspiration for an equally magnificent mural in the reception center at Rocky Reach Dam above Wenatchee.

The gist of the story was this: Billy Clapp, a lawyer of Ephrata, had proposed the plan. Once an ice dam had sent the Columbia River down the Grand Coulee. Why not build a man-made dam in the Columbia and send water into Grand Coulee again? That water could be used to irrigate a million or more acres.

There was one problem Billy Clapp and Rufus Woods did not know about. The bed of Grand Coulee was 600 feet higher than the bed of the Columbia River. The United States could not build a dam high enough to send water into Grand Coulee. If we did, the water behind the dam would back up into Canada, flood the land there, and probably bury a town or two. There would have to be two steps in getting water to Grand Coulee: first, a dam in the Columbia to raise the water as high as possible; then a pumping system to carry the water the rest of the way and pour it into the coulee.

The fight for Grand Coulee Dam began in 1918 and lasted until after 1933. The talk against it lasted even longer. In 1932 the Bureau of Reclamation outlined a plan for a dam that would furnish hydroelectric power and also operate a pumping system to carry water to Grand Coulee to irrigate land. They presented the plan to President Herbert Hoover. He turned it down because the country was in the middle of a depression. We did not need to spend money on any new irrigation projects, he said.

Many congressmen, especially those from the East, agreed with President Hoover. What would the Northwest do with all the power Grand Coulee

Dam would make? Put electric lights in gopher holes? The dam would be a white elephant!

But President Franklin Delano Roosevelt saw another side to the depression. Men needed work, and big federal projects would give them work. That belief was the beginning of many things, including two dams on the Columbia River. The Army Engineers started work on Bonneville Dam.

The Bureau of Reclamation began a survey of the river at Grand Coulee. There were many questions to answer: How deep would they have to dig to find bedrock? How big would the dam have to be to hold back the river at that place?

The engineers came up with some startling facts. Grand Coulee Dam was going to be the biggest single piece of masonry, or concrete, ever put together by man. The concrete in the dam would weigh over 22 million tons—enough concrete to make a 22-foot highway from Seattle to Miami, Florida, with a 3-foot sidewalk besides.

There were many things to do before they could start work on the dam. Grand Coulee was in the middle of nowhere. Roads and railroad tracks

Bureau of Reclamation

Grand Coulee Dam. Canal in center (arrow) carries water for irrigation.

must be built to bring in supplies. Towns must be built to house the workers.

It was late in 1935 before work started on the dam. First, just as at Bonneville, the engineers had to get rid of the river to have a place to work. And, just as at Bonneville, there was no hope of detouring the river through a tunnel or canal. Where the engineers planned to build the dam the river was more than 1,000 feet wide and rushing by at 14 miles an hour.

The engineers built cofferdams of huge steel tanks, 75 feet high, and they fastened them together with waterproof joints, enclosing 50 to 60 acres of the riverbed at a time. Then they pumped out the water and began to dig down to bedrock. They had to excavate 197 feet to strike bedrock.

More than once disaster threatened their work. When men and machines were excavating along the west bank, a million cubic yards of earth began sliding into the excavation. The engineers blocked the slide with everything they could lay their hands on. When they checked to find why the earth was sliding, they discovered a layer of wet clay beneath the slide. They dug tunnels far into the clay to drain off the water. At last the clay was dry. The slide stopped, and men could go on with their work.

Another slide occurred when men were working on the east bank. This time the whole slide was wet clay. At first the engineers were baffled. How could they stop it? Then one young engineer came up with an idea. Why not freeze the slide? They built a refrigeration plant, drove miles of ammonia pipes into the toe of the slide, froze it and kept it frozen while they worked.

The greatest threat of disaster did not come from a slide, but from the mighty river. One morning sirens warned of danger. A leak in the cofferdam! When the leak started, the river was 60 feet high and thundering through its channel.

All other work stopped. Men dumped everything they had at hand into the river above the leak, but with a *boom* a section of the cofferdam gave away and water roared in—40,000 gallons a minute.

Bureau of Reclamation

The canal below Long Lake Reservoir is paved by huge machines.

Men worked desperately, dumping hundreds of tons of rock, earth fill, tumbleweed, tangled wire, and even mattresses into the river to block the hole. At last they blocked it, repaired the cofferdam, pumped out the flood, and started work again.

The engineers had another problem, too—cooling the concrete as they built the dam. As concrete hardens, it shrinks and heats. Cooling the concrete in miles of highway does not present too much of a problem, because it is spread out and exposed to the air.

But the concrete in Grand Coulee Dam would not be spread out; it would be stacked up. Enough concrete to build a highway from Seattle to Miami was being stacked up, layer on layer. And each layer had to cool before the next layer was put on it. The engineers checked: It would take over 150 years for the concrete to cool naturally.

They built the dam in columns, pouring a depth of 5 feet of concrete at a time. In the concrete they buried miles of pipes and ran river water through the pipes to speed the cooling process. About 1,700 miles of pipes went into the dam.

During the years of work on the dam, many people still shouted about "all that power that would go to waste." To them, Grand Coulee was the white elephant of all time. But in 1941 the United States was catapulted into World War II. Then there was no talk of wasted power in the Northwest.

The United States needed planes; it takes aluminum to make planes; it takes electricity to make aluminum—10 kilowatt hours for every pound of aluminum.

The "useless" power of that "white elephant" in the Northwest helped furnish electricity for the aluminum for 60,000 planes. People of the Northwest knew that and were proud.

They did not know that Grand Coulee electricity was playing an even more vital part in winning the war. They did not know what was going on at a mysterious plant set down in the desert, south of Grand Coulee Dam. Army officers had come, looked over the place, and had told people in the little town of Hanford that the government needed the land. Then something began to happen

Bureau of Reclamation

This Columbia basin sprinkler waters 2½ acres every time it turns.

there—and in a terrific hurry. Workmen came in by the thousands.

Japan had surrendered before most people knew that the plant at Hanford had helped to build the atomic bomb.

People had thought of Grand Coulee Dam as a source of water for irrigation. Sale of electric power—if there was anybody to buy power in that wasteland—might someday help pay the cost of the dam. But irrigation was the main thing, they thought.

What happened was just the opposite. Throughout World War II, irrigation had to wait. After the war, engineers began building the plant for the irrigation system. They built two dams across the Ice Age bed of the Columbia River, making a lake 27 miles long. This was called an "equalizing reservoir" because it would keep a constant supply of water flowing through miles of canals, pipes, tunnels, and ditches in the irrigation system.

Grand Coulee Dam was outsize: 550 feet from bedrock to top, and 4/5ths of a mile long. It was built to produce almost two million kilowatts of electricity, but often produced more than two million. It was the greatest dam in North America.

Features of the irrigation project are outsize, too. Huge pumps raise the water from Roosevelt Lake behind the dam to the canal that leads to the reservoir. Each of these pumps can raise 1,600 second-feet of water—enough to supply a city the size of Chicago. In 1964, 6 pumps were in operation; 6 more pumps can be installed when they are needed. The feeder canal to the reservoir can carry 16,000 second-feet of water. One cement

Bureau of Reclamation

How irrigation changed the arid Columbia basin between 1952 and 1957.

pipe in the irrigation system, the Soap Lake Siphon, is more than 22 feet in diameter.

Grand Coulee Dam is an expensive project, but it is paying for itself. Before irrigation, most of the Columbia Basin was wasteland. Growth of towns in the basin shows what irrigation has meant: Pasco had fewer than 300 people in 1900; it had over 14,000 people in 1960. Moses Lake had a few more than 300 people in 1940; it had more than 11,000 people in 1960. But growth of towns does not tell the whole story, for much of the Columbia Basin is settled by farmers. In 1930 Grant County had fewer than 6,000 people; in 1963 it had over 49,000.

The one-time wasteland has helped the United States, too. In 1963 the people of the Columbia Basin paid about $28 million in federal taxes and another $7 million in state and local taxes. They paid that much when only one-third of the million acres of the Columbia Basin was being used.

8. "We Must Hang Together"

In 1775 the American colonies rebelled against Great Britain. The different colonies had been settled for different reasons, and the people in the different colonies did not see eye-to-eye about a lot of things. Now they would have to stop fighting among themselves and unite in the fight against Great Britain. Benjamin Franklin summed it up when he said, "Gentlemen, we must hang together, or they will hang us separately."

Men have learned to "hang together" in developing the power of the Columbia River. And that power is vast! A list of the fifteen largest hydroelectric plants in the world in operation in 1964 tells the story: Three of those plants are in Russia; eight are in the United States; six of the eight American plants are all on the Columbia River. Grand Coulee, The Dalles, and Chief Joseph get

Oregon State Highway Department

The Columbia River Gorge at Crown Point, 25 miles east of Portland.

their power from federal dams. The other three of those great hydroelectric plants on the Columbia River are not federal plants. They were built by PUDs—Public Utility Districts of the state of Washington. PUDs are consumer-owned organizations that build or buy dams and hydroelectric plants and market the power.

The Grant County PUD built Priest Rapids Dam and Wanapum Dam. Chelan County PUD built Rocky Reach Dam.

Besides being one of the world's largest hydroelectric plants, Rocky Reach has two very special features—a museum and a Fish Viewing Room.

The Columbia River flows past the big windows of the Fish Viewing Room. The windows have special lighting so that one can see the fish swimming by. Visitors can "look a salmon in the eye" as the fish swim upstream.

The second unusual feature at Rocky Reach is the archeological museum. This is how it happened: When engineers planned Rocky Reach Dam, they knew it would back up water and make a lake 43 miles long. This lake would cover a region where Indians had lived in long-past ages. Before water covered the region, archeologists came to survey and dig. Their diggings uncovered treasures 10,000 years old. These treasures are part of the archeological museum. Other displays trace the history of the region from those long-ago days, through pioneer times, to modern man.

Before there were federal dams in the Northwest, the power plants of the region were cooperating. They had formed the Northwest Power Pool to wheel power—to send it back and forth from one power plant to another where it was needed.

The first federal plant, at Bonneville, began operation in 1938. The government organized BPA—the Bonneville Power Administration—to market that power. BPA was to build power lines to send the power where it was needed. As other federal dams were built, BPA marketed that power, too. In 1954 BPA began cooperating with the non-federal power plants by letting them use BPA lines to send power to distant customers.

Being able to wheel power back and forth is important for hydroelectric plants. Waterpower is the cheapest power, but it does have its ups and downs. When water is high, a plant can furnish more power; when water returns to its usual level, the plant cannot furnish so much power. Engineers call the power they can be sure of, year around, "firm" power, and the high-water power "dump" power.

Oregon State Highway Department

Multnomah Falls drops 620 feet from a bluff in the Columbia Gorge.

American Museum of Natural History

The black bear was an early settler in the Columbia River region.

American Museum of Natural History

Deer are plentiful in the woods and fields bordering the Columbia.

Dump power is hard to sell. For instance, suppose you wanted to build a factory in the Northwest. You ask the head of a power plant, "How much power can you let me buy?"

Suppose he tells you, "I can let you have 10,000 kilowatts of firm power. Sometimes I can let you have 15,000 kilowatts. But I can let you have that extra 5,000 kilowatts on one condition: I can cut it off on seven days' notice."

You may say, "I can't run my factory that way. I'll contract for just 10,000 kilowatts."

So the power company will sell the 10,000 kilowatts; the other 5,000 kilowatts will probably go to waste.

BPA and the Northwest Power Pool changed that picture. Individual hydroelectric plants can borrow power when their supply is low and pay it back when their power is high.

But much power is still wasted on the Columbia River. At Grand Coulee Dam, during the spring floods, 135 million gallons of water a minute pour through the spillway of the dam. It makes a waterfall twice as high as Niagara Falls. Sightseers think it's a thrilling sight—and it is. Engineers think it doesn't need to be *quite* so thrilling. To them it's a sad waste of power. And not only Grand Coulee, but all the dams downriver below it, have to open their spillways when the spring floods come.

The Columbia River drains an area of over a

British Columbia Government

The forested Columbia, 33 miles from Golden in British Columbia.

quarter of a million square miles of land—much of it in snow-capped mountains. That is an area bigger than France, and more than twice as big as England, Scotland and Ireland. More than 150 rivers flow into the Columbia. Fourteen of those rivers can each pour more than one million gallons a minute into the Columbia. So there are dams on tributaries, and even on tributaries of tributaries.

But even all these dams cannot control the floods of the Columbia, for it is still a river of two nations. It rises in British Columbia, and more than half of its thundering descent from its headwaters is in falls and rapids in Canada. Only a joint international treaty could tame that part of the river.

The year 1964 brought two important breakthroughs in using the power of the Columbia River.

In September, the Columbia River Treaty was signed in Canada. Now Canada will build dams to help control the river on that side of the border. She will also let the United States build one dam that will back up water across the border between the two nations.

These treaty dams will regulate the flow of water into the United States, and they will add almost two million kilowatts of firm power to the dams below the border.

The second breakthrough in using the power of the Columbia River is in the building of Interties—long and very-high-power lines to connect the

Wide World Photos

Early explorers shot these boiling rapids above Grand Coulee Dam.

Pacific Northwest and the Pacific Southwest. These lines will carry a.c. (alternating current) and d.c. (direct current). There will be two 500,000-volt a.c. lines and two 750,000-volt d.c. lines. Those very-high-power d.c. lines are the first to be built in the United States and will be the longest in the world.

The d.c. lines are a breakthrough in themselves, for they can carry power more cheaply than a.c. lines. They do present one problem, though; the ground equipment used with them is very expensive, so only a very long d.c. line will pay for itself.

The Interties will save money for California and make money for the Northwest. Half of the power for California's utilities comes from steam generators, which burn oil or gas, and are much more expensive to operate. At any period when dump power is available in the Northwest, California may shut down the steam generators and use the cheaper hydroelectric power. When the Northwest sends a warning, "That's going to be all for a while," then California will start up the steam generators again.

These breakthroughs will cost millions—even billions—of dollars. But they will pay for themselves. Eleven states and two nations have said, "Gentlemen, we must hang together!"

And because they are hanging together they will reap more benefits from the Columbia—Powerhouse of North America.

Index